BRIGHT
IDEA
BOOKS

KU-757-709

A Plant THAT EATS Spiders: COOL FACTS ABOUT PLANTS

by Kaitlyn Duling

raintree

a Capstone company — publishers for children

Raintree is an imprint of Capstone Global Library Limited, a company incorporated in England and Wales having its registered office at 264 Banbury Road, Oxford, OX2 7DY – Registered company number: 6695582

www.raintree.co.uk
myorders@raintree.co.uk

Edited by Meg Gaertner
Designed by Becky Daum
Production by Colleen McLaren
Printed and bound in India

ISBN 978 1 4747 7461 1 (hardback)
ISBN 978 1 4747 8246 3 (paperback)

British Library Cataloguing in Publication Data
A full catalogue record for this book is available from the British Library.

Acknowledgements
We would like to thank the following for permission to reproduce photographs: iStockphoto: Boogich, 25, eefauscan, 20–21, javarman3, 5, lovleah, cover (background), OksanaRadchenko, 30–31, PeteMuller, 8, renacal1, 21, tonda, 12–13; Science Source: The Natural History Museum, London, 7; Shutterstock Images: AlessandroZocc, 17, Cathy Keifer, 16, Dudarev Mikhall, 11, 28, EcoPrint, 27, Hue Chee Kong, cover (foreground), MEDIAIMAG, 19, Michaelpuche, 15, Theerawan, 23, Todd Boland, 24–25
Every effort has been made to contact copyright holders of material reproduced in this book. Any omissions will be rectified in subsequent printings if notice is given to the publisher.

We would like to thank Jeff Conner, PhD, Professor of Plant Biology, for his help with this book.

CONTENTS

LET'S GET
Growing

Plants make it possible for humans to breathe. They provide medicine to heal people. Plants grow all around the world. There are about 400,000 different **species**. Each type is unique. Each plant is amazing.

The dragon blood tree is found in Yemen, on the Arabian Peninsula.

FLOWER
Power

Flowers are beautiful and colourful. They have been around for millions of years. The oldest known flower lived around 130 million years ago. Scientists found a **fossil** of the flower in Spain. They studied the fossil. The flower lived underwater. It lived among dinosaurs.

Scientists study plant fossils to see what plants were like long ago.

The moon flower is a type of morning glory.

MOONLIGHT ATTRACTION

Most flowers open during the day. Insects fly by. The insects take **pollen** from the flowers. Then the insects spread the pollen to other flowers. But moon flowers open only at night. They usually have large, white blossoms. The blossoms attract insects that come out at night.

SMELLY STALK

The corpse flower is a **rainforest** plant with a big stink. It is a huge **stalk** of many flowers. The corpse flower takes months to grow. Then it starts smelling like rotting flesh. The scent attracts flies. The flies land on the flower. They pick up its pollen. Then they spread the pollen to other plants. Luckily, the smell lasts only a day or two.

CHAPTER 3

AMAZING
Trees

There are more than 23,000 species of trees. The dragon blood tree gives off red **sap**. This "dragon blood" was used as medicine long ago.

Baobab trees look like water bottles. They act like them too. These trees can hold 300 litres (80 gallons) of water!

Baobab trees are found in Africa, the Arabian Peninsula and Australia.

THE NUMBERS

There are trillions of trees in the world. There are 400 times as many trees as there are humans!

ANCIENT GIANTS

Trees are the longest living organisms in the world. They can live for thousands of years. People count the rings in tree trunks. Each ring means one year of life. One tree in California, USA, is more than 5,000 years old!

DO NO HARM

Scientists used to cut down trees to study them. Today scientists use a special tool. They take out a sample of the tree's trunk. They count the rings on the sample.

Some of the oldest trees in the world are bristlecone pine trees.

CHAPTER 4

PLANTS FOR
Dinner

Humans have been growing food for thousands of years. They eat fruit and vegetables. They eat cereals. But some plants can be poisonous. People make rhubarb pie from the plant's stalks. But rhubarb leaves are poisonous.

Some vegetables have changed over the years. Most carrots used to be purple. In the 1500s, Dutch farmers bred orange carrots.

People can still buy purple carrots today.

Sundew plants curl around their meal.

Many animals eat plants. Some plants eat animals. A sundew plant has tiny, sticky hairs. These hairs trap flies. The Venus flytrap has an opening like a mouth. It closes around spiders, beetles or ants. These plants **digest** animals as food.

Venus flytraps can even catch grasshoppers!

CHAPTER 5

PLANTS THAT
Heal

Plants can be used for medicine. Aspirin is a drug. It helps with pain and fevers. Aspirin was first made from a **compound** in willow bark. Many plants have healing compounds.

One species
of poppy flowers is
used as a painkiller.

Cocoa beans are harvested to make chocolate and cocoa powder.

PLANT MEDICINE

Many medicines first came from plants. These medicines treat allergies. They fight disease. They help with swelling. Some plants make people numb. Other plants wake people up. Coffee and cocoa beans have **caffeine**. Some types of tea leaves do too.

Harvesters let cocoa beans dry in the sun.

CHAPTER 6

MANY
Habitats

Many plants grow in soil. But others grow underwater. Duckweed floats on water. It doesn't need soil to grow. It takes in **nutrients** from the Sun and water.

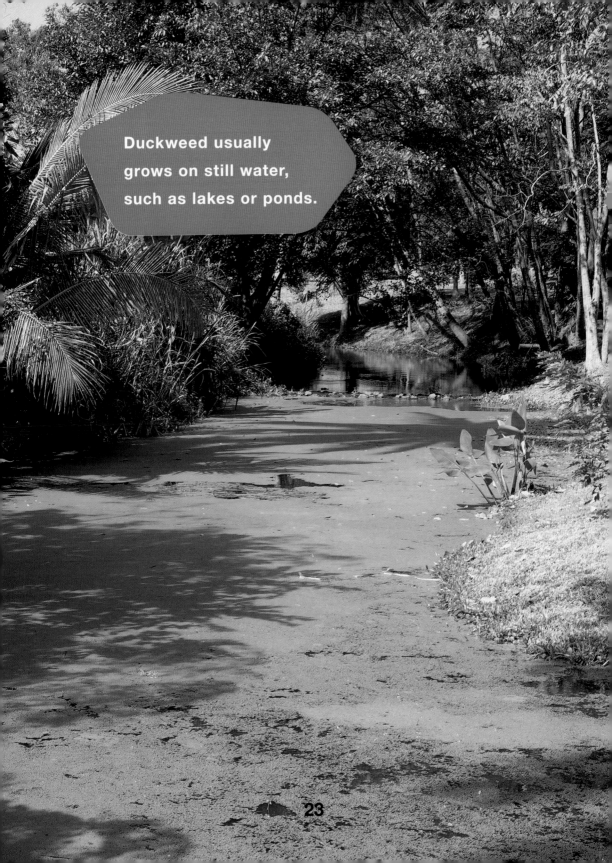

Duckweed usually grows on still water, such as lakes or ponds.

Air plants don't grow in soil. They don't grow in water either. They take in nutrients from the air. There are more than 500 species of air plants. They make good houseplants.

The roots of air plants latch on to whatever surface is around them.

Air plants have narrow, grass-like leaves.

CHAPTER 7

DESERT
Plants

The Rose of Jericho is a survivor.
It is called the **resurrection** plant.
Dry weather makes this plant curl up
like a ball. The plant waits for water.
Then it uncurls.

The *Welwitschia mirabilis* is a very weird plant. It grows in the desert. Its long leaves creep along the sand. It can live to be thousands of years old.

The *Welwitschia mirabilis* plant has only two leaves. They are torn apart by wind over time.

GLOSSARY

caffeine
a chemical that affects your brain and body and makes you more awake and active

compound
a chemical made of two or more substances

digest
to break down food

fossil
the image or remains of a living thing that has been preserved in rock or earth for a very long time

nutrient
a substance that is necessary for survival and growth

pollen
a powdery substance used by flowering plants to spread themselves

rainforest
a dense forest that receives heavy rainfall throughout much of the year

resurrection
the act of coming back to life

sap
a mix of water and minerals that moves through plants

species
a group of plants or animals of the same kind that can produce offspring together

stalk
the main stem of a plant

TRIVIA

1. Black walnut trees produce a toxin. The toxin seeps into the soil. It hurts and sometimes kills nearby plants. Humans and animals are not affected by it.

2. Ripe cranberries bounce and float in water. They have small pockets of air inside. Old cranberries do not float.

3. The world's tallest known tree is a redwood called Hyperion. It towers over the other trees in Redwood National Park in California, USA. It is 115 metres (379 feet) tall. That is twice the height of New York City's Statue of Liberty from base to torch!

4. Herbs and spices are both used in cooking. But they are different. Herbs come from the leafy part of a plant. Spices come from a plant's bark, flower, seed or fruit.

ACTIVITY

GROWING AT HOME

You can grow plants without even leaving your house. Make your own garden using soil, seeds and clear plastic cups.

1. Add potting soil and vegetable seeds to a clear plastic cup.

2. Place your cup by a window where it will receive a lot of sunlight. Spray in a little water occasionally. Watch the seedlings grow.

You can keep a field journal. Record what happens to the plant each day. You can write or draw to describe what you see.

FIND OUT MORE

Ready to learn more about amazing plants?

Books

Killer Plants and Other Green Gunk (Disgusting and Dreadful Science), Anna Claybourne (Franklin Watts, 2017)

The Wacky World of Living Things!, Melvin Burger (Scholastic, 2017)

What On Earth? Trees, Kevin Warwick (QED Publishing, 2018)

Websites

BBC Bitesize: Plants
www.bbc.com/bitesize/topics/zy66fg8

DK Find Out!: Plants
www.dkfindout.com/uk/animals-and-nature/plants/

INDEX